PRESENTED TO:

FROM:

EVANGELISM'S FLIPSIDE

A Journey of Reaping the Unexpected

By

JOHN JAY RICCI

Copyright © 2019 by John Jay Ricci
All Rights Reserved
Printed in the United States of America

REL006201: Religion: Biblical Studies - Topical

ISBN 978-1-7339247-0-2

All Scripture quotes are from the King James Bible

No part of this work may be reproduced without the expressed consent of the publisher, except for brief quotes, whether by electronic, photocopying, recording, or information storage and retrieval systems.

Address All Inquiries To:
THE OLD PATHS PUBLICATIONS, Inc.
142 Gold Flume Way
Cleveland, Georgia, U.S.A.
E-mail: TOP@theoldpathspublications.com

Distributors and other information here:
Web: www.theoldpathspublications.com

1.0

Contents

Dedication 5
Introduction 6
Chapter 1: When Your Light Shines 13
Chapter 2: One New Year's Eve 20
Chapter 3: While at a Train Station 22
Chapter 4: A Strange Encounter 59
Chapter 5: Logan Airport 62
Chapter 6: In the Air 69
Chapter 7: Miami Airport 72
Chapter 8: Belize! 74
Conclusion 85
Action Steps 86
Endnotes 90
About the Author 93

Dedication

This is my first book on this subject and I want to dedicate it above all else to my Lord and Saviour Jesus Christ, God's precious Son whose love and grace towards me made this all possible. I also dedicate this to the late Barbara A. Ricci, my beloved mom whose selfless love, sacrifice and investment in my life paved the way for a project like this to come to fruition. Finally, I dedicate this to the rest of my family, friends and the faithful men and women of God past and present who have been a great blessing and encouragement as I sought the furtherance of the everlasting gospel.

Introduction

In the New Testament, Hebrews 10:24 says, *"And let us consider one another to provoke unto love and to good works."* The Greek term for *provoke* comes from the root *paroxuno* which means "to sharpen alongside; to stir up." I want to assure you I am not claiming to have "arrived" and the Lord knows that I do not see myself as an expert evangelist. So while I seek to stir up my fellow saints I will also get sharpened along the way. My twofold purpose in writing this book is first to help Christians to *recognize* and then *seize* the opportunities right in front of them so they can enjoy a benefit of evangelism that much of Christendom has largely forgotten about today.

Too many of us have inoculated ourselves from the exploits awaiting us because we have convinced ourselves to accept the lie that because soul winning is a command of our Lord, then by default it must be dull or boring. My goal throughout this book is to show you otherwise. As you read about the adventures I've been on and the fruit it has stirred, not just around me, but *in* me, my prayer is that it will likewise produce a desire in you to open your own evangelism treasure chest. Bible believers know that taking part in the Great Commission as a soul winner is not an option but a responsibility. However, I do not think Christians should obey out of guilt or even out of fear of divine chastisement as these are very poor motivators. We ought to obey out of *love* for our Saviour and for the expectation of the heavenly power and joy we will overflow with too! Sadly, in many Christian circles today there seems to be a "hands-off" approach to reaching people for Christ. These Christians want to show the gospel in their behavior instead of telling the gospel with their words. I believe these Christians are cutting their blessings short when they take this approach. Not only this, but it is not biblical to reduce the Great Commission to "lifestyle evangelism" or a "social gospel" as if to assume the lost will someday "sense" their need of salvation solely by watching a Christian live their life. In addition, this is not the method Jesus Himself used. Our Lord didn't wait six months or longer to "win over" people like Nicodemus or the woman at the well with His godly lifestyle, but He *spoke* the gospel to them the *same* day He met them (John 3:1-21; 4:5-29). Should we do any less?

The Bible teaches that faith comes by hearing the Word of God (Rom 10:17). In clear passages such as Ezekiel 3:18, Acts 4:20, 18:9 (and more) God plainly tells us to *speak* the truth in love to people so they will hear about the wonderful gift of salvation He wants them to have.

Someone may object here and claim Jesus gave the Great Commission only to the Apostles, and therefore it doesn't apply to Christians today. This objection fails

INTRODUCTION

because Jesus told His Apostles that they were to go into all nations and make disciples and to teach their disciples to make more disciples and their disciples to make even more disciples on and on until the end of human history (Matt 24:14; 28:19-20). The Apostles themselves would die long before that time would come yet Jesus said He wanted the gospel preached all over the world until then. Thus He was giving clear instructions that wouldn't just apply to the first century Apostles, but to all Christian disciples since then. Do you claim to be a Christian and thus a disciple (follower) of Christ? If yes, then the Great Commission applies to you as it did the Apostles.

Another popular objection is: "We have to meet people's physical needs to earn the right to preach the gospel to them." Nowhere does the Bible teach that we have to "earn" such a right. Since Christ commanded us to preach the gospel to the lost, with that command comes the authorization as well, so we really do not have to wait for anyone else to give that to us! Furthermore, we do not see Jesus, the master soul winner waiting to "earn" the right before preaching the gospel to the lost souls around Him. In fact, on at least one occasion, it was only *after* three days of preaching that Jesus gave the people something to eat (Matt 15:32) because He wanted to emphasize the importance of proclaiming the gospel. Please don't misunderstand me here. Neither I nor the Bible is saying that living a godly life isn't important or that we shouldn't try to meet the temporal needs of people when possible. However, we must not prioritize the temporal *over* the eternal. Christians need to remember that it is vitally important that we give the lost an invitation to accept the gospel of Christ as that is God's primary focus.

Often we forget that our Lord's commands (especially concerning evangelism) are meant to fill up our joy not take it away. My desire in writing this book is to help change your perspective on soul winning and the Great Commission from: *we have to* instead to: *we get to*. Beloved, our Lord didn't give you commands to ruin your life, but to *enhance* it (John 10:10). Notice here in John 15:10-11 Jesus said, *"If ye keep my commandments, ye shall abide in my love; even as I have kept my Father's commandments, and abide in his love. These things have I spoken unto you, that my joy might remain in you, and that your joy might be full."*

Under the Old Covenant, God gave commandments to His people for their benefit (Deut 6:24) and it is no different for Christians under the New Covenant. God has orchestrated it in such a way that when we obey His command to be His witnesses, it is *we* who will have cause for celebration and rejoicing. The encounter between Philip the evangelist and the Ethiopian eunuch is a good example of this. After Philip preached the gospel to the eunuch, and the eunuch got saved and

INTRODUCTION

baptized, the Bible says in Acts 8:39 that *"when they were come up out of the water, the Spirit of the Lord caught away Philip, that the eunuch saw him no more: and he went on his way rejoicing."*

Someone may say, "Sure there's a reason to rejoice when people respond to the gospel and you're getting results, but how can you rejoice when nobody responds and you get no results?" While seeing results from your soul winning efforts is a reason to rejoice, the Bible shows us it is not the only reason to rejoice. Just because you don't get a positive response to the gospel doesn't mean you can't rejoice. In Acts chapter five, the Apostles got assaulted and jailed for preaching the gospel. They weren't seeing a lot of results, especially from the religious rulers (whom they were also trying to reach for Christ) right? However, after the religious leaders had the Apostles beaten Scripture says *"they departed from the presence of the council, rejoicing that they were counted worthy to suffer shame for his name"* (Acts 5:41). So although the circumstances for the Apostles weren't pleasant, and they weren't seeing the results they wanted, they still had reason to be brimming with joy! Despite the persecution and the lack of results, the Apostles rejoiced because their obedience to the Great Commission took them on an adventure, and through it, they glorified God's name.

Just like the Apostles, in order for today's Christians to get and stay enthusiastic about the huge task of world evangelization, we must view each evangelism opportunity, not as another burden to carry but as a new adventure to experience. In Matthew 9:37-38 Jesus said, "The harvest truly is plenteous, but the labourers are few; Pray ye therefore the Lord of the harvest, that he will send forth labourers into his harvest." So while I certainly believe in praying for more laborers I also believe in putting feet to my prayers and through this book, I am doing just that. I have a burden to see more Christians get passionate about what Jesus Himself was most passionate about, lost souls. It seems like the colder our Western society gets towards the things of God the more standoffish Christians get towards evangelizing it. But only fired-up Christians will melt the block of ice separating our society from the biblical gospel. It should be that the colder the society gets, the hotter our Christian witness gets. I'd like to encourage more Christians to not just obey the Great Commission out of duty, but be expecting to evangelize the next lost person God brings into their lives. I really like the book of Acts because it chronicles the adventures the early Christians experienced as they faithfully obeyed God's Great Commission mandate. In Acts chapter fifteen, while on their missionary journey to Jerusalem, Paul and Barnabas *"passed through Phenice and Samaria, declaring the conversion of the Gentiles: and they caused great joy unto all the brethren. And when they were come to Jerusalem, they were received of the church, and of the apostles and elders, and they declared all things that God had done with them"* (Acts 15:3-4).

Just by sharing what God had done with and for them while they were out witnessing, Paul and Barnabas had

INTRODUCTION

brought great joy and excitement to the brethren in their day. In this book with God's help, I too seek to do the same for my generation today. Now let's notice again the phrase *"all things that God had done with them"*. This isn't only referring to the "conversion of the Gentiles" (i.e. what God did in and for the unsaved) but it also includes what God was doing in and through the saved (in this case Paul and Barnabas). From my experience, most Christians don't see evangelism as a two-sided coin that has blessings on both sides. Instead, most treat it like a one-sided coin and only focus on what God is doing in the lives of the lost they're trying to reach (or have reached) with the Gospel. Unfortunately, when this happens, Christians end up overlooking what's happening on the flipside. I hope to show in this book (through some personal stories) the types of joys and blessings simultaneously available on the *other* side of evangelism so believers can be inspired to be expecting and reaping these blessings in their own lives as well.

My prayer for you, dear reader and fellow saint in the Lord, is that you would not settle for only being excited about what God does in the lives of the unsaved you reach with the Gospel. But may you be equally excited or more so with what He will do in you, for you and through you as the Great Commission becomes a great commitment in your life. And to put feet to my prayers, I now share my adventures from the soul-winning trails so that you too may see the great things God has done.

When Your Light Shines

"To be a soul winner is the happiest thing in this world."[1]

Charles H. Spurgeon

Any student of the Bible knows that God says we are wise when we are soul winners (Prov 11:30) which is another term for being "fishers of men" (Matt 4:19). We can accomplish this using several creative methods. One of these ways is through public, open-air street evangelism which godly men of the past, such as George Whitefield and John Wesley did as well as the Lord Jesus and His Apostles.

One day, after a church service I met a Jewish Christian named Ben through Mike, our mutual Christian brother who (at the time) was heading off to Bible college. I discovered that Ben also loves to do open-air street ministry as I do, and we are an encouragement to one another since very few Christians today desire to do this front-line evangelism. Sadly, many Christians in this Laodicean (lukewarm) church age would rather keep their faith inside the walls of a church building and expect the lost to come to them than go out seeking the lost *where they are* like the Lord Jesus Himself did. Since Ben and I (at the time of this writing) live in Massachusetts, we coordinated a plan to meet together to do evangelism throughout the streets of downtown Boston, or Harvard Square in Cambridge or any other area with high foot traffic as the Lord would lead. Though (at the time of this writing) I use some creative witnessing tools that Open Air Campaigners, a local church/non-profit mission provides evangelists and occasionally team up with their local staff to do soul winning, I am not yet serving in evangelism full time, I still have a full-time secular job as does Ben. I still have a full-time secular job as does Ben. He has his own business and sometimes his schedule is different and more flexible than mine and he can get out to the streets before I am.

One day he was in downtown Boston with another Christian brother and together they were handing out tracts and witnessing. As they were doing this, a man named John approached him, and John told him he too was a Christian. He told them that just by seeing Ben out here giving out tracts; God had used this to convict John that he too needs to be out here doing this. Then three weeks later, while I was out doing street evangelism with Ben, John shows up in Boston again and greets Ben, and then Ben introduces John and then John joins us in passing out tracts! Then a short while later that evening, while John is giving tracts away, a man named Eli walks up to him. Eli is also a Christian and was in the area looking for a job. God used our example of being obedient to His Great Commission and this instantly convinces Eli (who had his Bible in his bag as well) that he should also join us as we hand out gospel tracts and witness for the Lord Jesus. So although Ben, John, Eli and I are involved in different churches outside of Boston, we all have the same burden for the souls of Boston and God has brought us together to encourage each other in soul winning. We still do street evangelism together as much as our schedules permit. None of us claims to be perfect, but as we strive together to further the gospel, Scripture tells us *"iron sharpeneth iron"* (Prov 27:17). Many Christians know that the *"harvest truly is plenteous but the labourers are few"* (Matt 9:37). And these same Christians pray for the Lord to *"send forth more labourers into his harvest"* (Matt 9:38) but when we put feet to our prayers head out to the harvest and *expect* more gospel workers, God *will* deliver in astounding ways! It was just amazing how He brought four Christians from different church backgrounds together to seek the lost, and it all began when each of us stepped out in obedient faith and let our individual candles burn bright. *"Let your light so shine before men, that they may see your good works, and glorify your Father which is in heaven"* (Matt 5:16). Praise the Lord (**PTL**)!

> *"I would rather win souls than be the greatest king or emperor on earth; I would rather win souls than be the greatest general that ever commanded an army; I would rather win souls than be the greatest poet, or novelist, or literary man who ever*

walked the earth. My one ambition in life is to win as many as possible."[2]

R. A. Torrey

One Monday in December while I was at my 9-5 job in Boston I anticipated going soul winning with Ben (the Christian brother I mentioned earlier). The plan was to head to the famous Harvard Square in Cambridge, MA to do street ministry which would include open proclamation using an amplifier, handing out gospel tracts and getting into as many personal conversations as possible. Ben headed to Harvard Square ahead of me since he had the day off from work and I would meet him there after I finished work, but around 3 pm I got a text message on my phone from Ben saying he had to cancel because his brother's car had broken down. His brother and brother's girlfriend were stuck in Vermont, and he needed to drive up there and pick them up. So Ben had to leave Harvard Square to head up there, but the good news for Ben was that although he couldn't meet up with me, he would have three hours in the car to preach the gospel to his brother and his brother's girlfriend, both of whom were unsaved. I was excited for him, but a little disappointed because Ben's zeal for the Lord was an encouragement for me and it was a blessing to have him as a soul-winning partner. It would also bitterly cold outside this evening so that added to my disappointment. But then I sent a text message to two other Christian brothers, John, and Eli (whom I mentioned earlier), to see if they were up to coming out to Harvard Square with me. If I found no one else to join me I was ready to head home and attend to other things. But then I got a response from John saying he was up for some street evangelism, however, instead of Harvard Square he wanted to meet up in downtown Boston (on the Boston Commons just outside the Park Street train station). So I agreed, and when I met him there after work he had his two children, his wife and a women's leader from his church with him. His wife and this woman had a big pot of soup, and while we were doing evangelism, they went around serving soup to the homeless in the area that evening. Although John had brochures from his church (which at the time of this writing is a Pentecostal church) he encouraged his children to give out the gospel tracts from my church I brought with me. After I did a little open-air preaching, Eli showed up with his Bible, and he joined us in ministry, which was an extra blessing for sure. Though it was bitterly cold, we were all on fire for God that evening. By now it was around 7 pm and just before finishing up for the night and heading home, we met a homeless couple named Kevin and Michelle near an outdoor fruit cart. Boy did they have a story to tell! Kevin said that earlier in the day he stumbled upon an old silver dollar coin. At this point in their lives, he and his pregnant girlfriend Michelle were homeless and hungry and they were tempted to steal some food in order to eat. But then he felt God telling him that He would supply their needs. Kevin also said that he somehow knew that God was going to send someone to tell him more about Him. So Kevin got the idea that he should take the coin to some coin dealers in the Boston area and get the best price. After being offered three dollars by one dealer and five dollars by another dealer, he found a place that would give him eighteen dollars for the coin which he accepted. He used the money and bought some food for him and his girlfriend. Then God brought us together at the fruit stand, which was near the train station I was just about to enter to head home for the evening. Had I left, I wouldn't have been able to witness what happened next. We started talking to Kevin and Michelle about their eternal destiny. Kevin said he believed in some "higher power" (whom he called God) but wasn't sure what he believed about Jesus. Then John's wife, who had met up with us (after going around and serving soup to the homeless) also offered Kevin and Michelle a bowl of soup and they each gladly received the soup since they were very hungry and that is why they were at that fruit art in the first place. So while they were there eating the hot soup, I opened my New Testament and began to talk with them about God's simple plan of salvation. Then Eli (who also had his Bible) showed them Romans 10:9 and asked them if they wanted to receive the gift of eternal life by placing their trust in Jesus. Kevin and Michelle affirmed that they did and right there Eli prayed with them as they publicly confessed their trust in Christ. After asking them some follow-up questions, the women's leader from John's church obtained their contact information to make arrangements to further assist and disciple them.

What began as a disappointing day turned into rejoicing by the end of the evening. I was all set to go home after work, a little discouraged because my soul winning partner had to cancel on me. Although Ben's zeal for evangelism is an encouragement, God showed me that ultimately I needed to rely on Him and His power alone. So by faith, I resolved to go and God brought John, Eli and the others to come alongside me that evening. And as a result, two more people came to trust Jesus for salvation and enter the family of God. Once again, the Lord showed me He is not looking for a person's ability, but their availability. Jesus said, "go ye" (Mark 16:15) and if we will just obey, He will do the rest. **PTL!**

One New Year's Eve

"If you have no joy, there's a leak in your Christianity somewhere."[3]

Billy Sunday

One New Year's evening I joined up with a pastor friend of mine from Salem, MA, who had his son and one of his faithful men from their church alongside him. We were open-air preaching on the Commons in downtown Boston during the "First Night" activities. It was a bitterly cold night, as it usually is for this time of the year, and there were multitudes of people around to ring in the New Year. While we were there preaching using our portable voice amplifiers, we got swarmed by at least nine or ten self-proclaimed homosexual women. They were obliviously drunk and yelling at us and trying to prevent us from preaching. One woman even pulled her pants down to flash us, but we looked away so we didn't see the perversion. However, as they were making a scene, a group of about seven teenagers stopped to observe what was going on. Seeing an opportunity, I engaged all seven in a gospel conversation. Several of the teens admitted that they had never previously spoken to anyone about Christ before. To some of you reading this book it may shock you to learn that there are *still* plenty of people in America who have not heard the biblical gospel even once. One boy in this group who never heard the good news before was a Catholic, so it was a blessing to plant the seed of the gospel with him. After I finished talking to them, they left and I noticed the homosexuals were still there heckling the pastor. Because of these hecklers getting louder and vulgar two other teenage girls stopped in front of me to observe the scene just long enough for me to talk to them about where they would spend eternity. It is interesting to note here that, when I arrived in Boston that evening to join the pastor and his team, though there were many people around, most weren't interested in talking about spiritual things at first. But then when the homosexuals raided our space and came to heckle us, God used their foolishness to draw over those interested in talking just long enough for me to give them the gospel. Apparently, the Devil thought bringing the homosexuals over to us would shut down the preaching of the gospel, but in fact, God turned it around and used it for us to see even *more* people hear the gospel, not less. The Enemy's plan backfired as he planned mischief against God's people, yet it returned upon his own head (Psalm 7:14-16). **PTL!**

While at a Train Station

"The Great Commission is the Great Adventure of Christianity"[4]

Ron Luce

One cold and rainy Monday evening in January, my soul-winning partner Ben and I went to a train station in the city of Malden, Massachusetts (which is about fifteen minutes from Boston). We had with us a colorful gospel display board measuring about two feet long and about one and a half feet wide. Mounted on wood with legs that folded down, it stood horizontally and the caption at the top of this display said, "See Three Things God Has Never Seen." Then just below the caption were three doors which read from left to right. The first door said: "God has never seen a person that has not sinned." Then just below this door was Romans 3:23 which says, *"For all have sinned, and come short of the glory of God."* The second door read: "God has never seen a person that He does not love." Then right below this was John 3:16 which says, *"For God so loved the world, that he gave his only begotten Son, that whosoever believeth in him should not perish, but have everlasting life."* The third and final door said: "God has never seen a person He cannot save." Then just below this was Romans 10:13 which says, *"For whosoever shall call upon the name of the Lord shall be saved."* We got this attractive display board from a gospel ministry (at the time of this writing) called Fishers of Men International in Connecticut, MA.

Ben and I had planned to go to the station and just display the sign hoping that people who had nothing better to do but wait for their bus to arrive would be intrigued by "three things God has never seen" and come over to talk with us. We were not there five minutes when the Devil tried to disrupt and discourage our witness. A Massachusetts Bay Transportation Authority (MBTA) train official came over and asked us if we had a permit and if we didn't, we had to leave. I politely explained to her that another MBTA Inspector whom I had spoken to prior to coming here, told me that MBTA security had given clearance for people like us to be here as long as we respected their policy guidelines which we were. I even offered to give her the other Inspector's badge number to assure her we wanted to obey the rules and not be disruptive. But she told us she didn't know the other MBTA official to whom I was referring and that she would check with her supervisor, and if her supervisor said no, then we would have to go. So as soon as she left we bowed our heads right there at the station and we prayed to our Heavenly Father. We told the Lord we believed He wanted us there at the station that night, but we put this situation in His hands and if He wanted us to we would leave. After we prayed we heard nothing more from the official, she never came back and told us we had to leave. In fact, she walked by us several times during the evening, but she didn't say a word, she just ignored us. So God clearly wanted us there, and He made sure we were allowed to stay there and give out the gospel through this attractive gospel display we had. After God removed the barriers Satan tried to put in our way, Ben and I had a great night of evangelism.

We were there at the station during "rush hour" when people were heading home after work or school. We began the night by having each of the three doors of the display hidden behind separate pieces of white paper to increase the intrigue, to draw people to want to see "three things God has never seen." It worked, as we had several people come up to us. A Muslim man came over and he wanted to see what this was all about. So I asked him if he wanted to see three things God has never seen and he shook his head in the affirmative. So I showed him the first door: God has never seen a person that has not sinned. Then I showed the Romans 3:23 verse under it which says, *"For all have sinned, and come short of the glory of God."* I asked him if he knew what sin was and he said no, which surprised me because I assumed that as a Muslim he would at least know what sin was. But apparently, he was a Muslim in name only, and there are a few of those. So I explained that sin was anything against God's Law such as lying, stealing, adultery and so forth. Then I asked this Muslim man if he ever told a lie before and he said no, again much to my surprise. I then pointed to the "all" in Romans 3:23 and asked him if he believed that the "all" in "all have sinned" included him. Perhaps feeling the conviction of the Holy Spirit, he conveniently said he had to leave. Now Jesus told us to go fish for men (Matt 4:19) but He never said we would catch every fish. He expects us always to be faithful (Matt 25:21) not fruitful. God is the one who gives the increase (1 Cor 3:6-7) therefore the results are up to Him. So although the Muslim man didn't stick around, God brought another man named Jimmy up to our gospel display. He was looking to use Ben's phone to make a phone call, and he was also looking for some money. Seeing an opportunity, I told Jimmy that we would help him if he would let us show him "three things God has never seen." We were ready to help Jimmy even if he didn't want us to talk to him about the Lord. But in Matthew 10:16 Jesus told us to be *"wise as serpents, and harmless as doves"* so I saw a chance to turn this situation into an opportunity to give the gospel. After Jimmy used Ben's phone to make a call, we had his attention. We took him through the three doors and he confessed openly that he was a sinner and needed God's forgiveness. He then let Ben lead him to Christ right there and then!

A little while after this divine appointment, we removed the white paper and allow people to just read the display uncovered. Many eyes looked at our sign and its gospel message as people were walking in and out of the station and although many didn't stop to talk, I know that God's Word will not return void (Isaiah 55:11). He promises it will impact their hearts in one way or another. Besides being able to give the gospel to the lost, God sent a Spanish family of believers to us so we could mutually encourage each other. Shortly after this, God used our gospel display to draw an interesting Christian man named Ricardo over to us. He was a middle-aged man who said he had gotten saved a while ago and through his line of work God allowed him to meet many cable TV news personalities. Ricardo showed Ben and me pictures on his cell phone of famous people I recognized from CNN and other "mainstream" news outlets he had his photo taken with. Ben and I also learned that though Ricardo was already saved his wife sadly was unsaved and still trapped in the false religion of Islam. So Ben and I gave Ricardo a DVD about soul winning and a gospel tract, specifically tailored to reach Muslims, hoping to help his wife see the error of Islam and to put her trust in Christ instead. I also gave him the address to my church and invited him to come. We then prayed with and for Ricardo right there at the train station and he thanked us for being out here shining the gospel light. The Apostle Paul told Timothy *"Let no man despise thy youth; but be thou an example of the believers, in word, in conversation, in charity, in spirit, in faith, in purity"* (1st Tim 4:12). We are to be an example to other Christians and perhaps there's no better way to do this than to follow Christ unashamedly by fishing for men. By committing to be a soul seeker for Jesus (and enjoying it) we can encourage other brethren to do likewise. **PTL!**

> *"I don't believe you're going to have real joy until you begin to do the will of God."[5]*
>
> Lester Roloff

Ben and I met at the Sullivan Square train station in the city of Somerville (a city close to Boston) because it was raining on this Tuesday evening. We were originally planning to go to the Harvard Square MBTA train station in Cambridge. But thankfully at the last minute, the Lord changed our plans. As Proverbs 16:9 says, *"A man's heart deviseth his way: but the LORD directeth his steps."* Though Ben and I knew Harvard Square (and other locations) needs the gospel, in hindsight we were glad we followed the leading of the Holy Spirit to go to Sullivan Square instead. This station had a canopy over the front doors which protected us and our gospel display signs from the rain. Before we began our night of witnessing, we bowed our heads right there at the station and Ben led us in prayer as we asked the Lord for His protection, His power and for Him to let us have a fruitful evening. We had a wonderful night of witnessing as the Lord brought to us the people He had already prepared for us to talk to. He also brought Christians across our path for mutual encouragement. Ben and I again brought with us the "Three Things God Has Never Seen" sign which we also used at a previous train station. Besides the "Three Things..." sign, Ben had made up a smaller white sign which included a partial quote of John 14:6 where Jesus said, *"I am the way, the truth and the life."* And on the bottom of his smaller sign was the question in blue lettering "Need prayer?" in the left-hand corner. It was the evening rush hour, and we picked a corner at the station where we stood posted with our signs, waiting on the Lord to provide us with opportunities to have some redemptive conversations. As I mentioned earlier, the policy of the MBTA train stations is that as long as patrons approached us and we aren't aggressively approaching them with our gospel materials, and we do not cause a disturbance or block the flow of foot traffic, we could stay on the premises. Ben and I also had plenty of Bible tracts and DVDs to hand to those who approached us and showed an interest in the gospel. In the first few minutes of standing at the station with our signs, Ben struck up a conversation with a man who was sitting on a bench there. As he was talking to him a dark-skinned man named Charles, perhaps in his 40s approached me and squinted his eyes as he was reading the sign. I waved him to come closer and then asked him if he'd like to see three things God has never seen. He said yes, so I took him through the three doors. I began with the first door which said: "God has never seen a person that has not sinned." Then I showed him the corresponding verse just beneath it from Romans 3:23 which says, *"For all have sinned, and come short of the glory of God."* I asked Charles if he understood what sin was. He nodded his head to affirm that indeed he did. But as soul winners, we don't just want to get the prospect to understand sin in a broad sense; we want to bring it closer to home. We want the prospect to not only understand that *everyone* is a sinner, but also understand that he *personally* is a sinner as well. So to make sure he understood what sin was, I asked him if he would give me an example of sin. I asked him if lying and stealing are examples of sin. He said yes and then I asked Charles if he has ever told a lie. He said yes and then I asked him if he's ever stolen anything and again he said he had. I then pointed to the word "all" in Romans 3:23 and asked if he agreed that he is included in the "all"? He agreed that he is included in the "all." Believing that Charles correctly understood his sinful condition before a holy God, I moved on to the next door and then to the third and final door.

As soon as I showed Charles Romans 10:13 which says, *"Whosoever shall call upon the name of the Lord shall be saved"* he got a call on his cell phone which he said he had to take. But as he was walking away, he thanked me for showing him the truth and he took a gospel tract for the road. So I was a little disappointed that Charles had to go before I could ask him if he wanted to repent and trust Christ but I was happy that he was interested enough to take a gospel tract with him. We cannot always see people get saved right in front of our eyes, and that's not our responsibility either, because we can't save the person. The Holy Spirit of God gives the increase, and He uses His Word to do it because it is quick and powerful.

Charles heard me verbally share the gospel with him and also walked away with that gospel tract, so he definitely had enough information to get saved if he wanted to. A few minutes after Charles left, a young woman named Tanya stopped by to look at the sign. She read the title "Three Things God Has Never Seen" and I waved her over to come closer to talk about it. When she came over, I asked her "Have you ever seen anything like this before?" She shook her head signaling she had not. So I walked her through the three doors. When I finished with the third door, Tanya professed that she had already put her trust in Jesus Christ as Saviour. She said she just moved to the area. She had been in a turbulent relationship and was now looking for a good church. Upon hearing those words, we gave her some gospel material and told her about a good church to look into. She was smoking a cigarette while I was talking to her, and I asked her if she thought the Lord would want her to stop smoking and she admitted that she needed to get the victory over that sinful habit. I told her of a Bible-based addiction program that would equip her to get the victory over cigarettes and she was delighted to receive the information. As she left to get on her bus, she thanked us for taking the time to talk with her. It is evident that God was working in Tanya's heart and He had given her a desire to look for a biblical church. If Ben and I had not obeyed the Lord and went out soul winning *that* night at *that* train station we would not have been able to meet and encourage Tanya and point her toward a biblical church. And perhaps she would've met and been led astray by the Jehovah's Witnesses (JWs) who have been there at that same station trying to recruit those seeking spiritual answers into their cult. In the gospel of Matthew, Jesus told His people He wanted them to make disciples of all nations not just make converts (28:19-20). I want to encourage soul winners to carry gospel tracts with them and to make sure that the tracts have a contact address or phone number on them so that prospects can reach out if they are interested in finding a biblical church. Sometimes when I'm in downtown Boston on lunch break from work, I see Christians passing out tracts and when time permits, I walk over to them, take their tract and thank them for caring for the eternal destiny of lost souls. Most of the time these Christians have biblically sound tracts, but when I look I often find no contact information on the back of the tract available for the recipient. So I try to encourage them to put contact information on the back of the next batch of tracts they plan to hand out. We as Christians must remember that the Great Commission as outlined by Jesus is not just about seeing people get saved, but also making it easy for them to be followed up and discipled. **PTL!**

> **"God has many special blessings for the Christian who works hard to win souls."**[6]
>
> C.L. Cagan

After we spoke with Tanya, we got to witness to two men who approached us in succession, one named Junior and another man a few minutes later named José. Now if you remember that we were at a bus and train station, and buses were coming and going, so in between our conversations with people, Ben and I held up our signs and stood there looking like fools for Jesus. I'm not saying Ben, and I are fools for shining as lights in the world as that's exactly what Jesus told us to be (Matthew 5:14-16). While we were standing there in between conversations, the people who didn't want to approach us and talk just watched us from a distance with a bewildered look on their faces. One group of teenagers was giggling and talking as they kept looking over towards us. As Christians, it does not surprise us when the lost look at us as if we're fools because the Bible already told us that *"the preaching* [proclaiming or publishing] *of the cross is to them that perish foolishness"* (1 Cor 1:18). That is fine with us because the rest of the verse says, *"unto us which are saved it is the power of God."* To the world, we looked like fools out there holding up gospel signs on a rainy cold winter night during rush hour. However, before we began we prayed, got filled with God's power and died to self so it didn't bother us. Dead people don't get distracted or offended. Therefore, when Christians die to themselves, it will only matter what Christ thinks; not with what the world thinks. So it was fine with us that to the lost we looked like fools for Jesus because we know that great is our reward in heaven!

As I mentioned, Ben had walked over to talk to someone who was sitting down on a bench a few feet away from where I was standing. As he was talking and holding his sign, about eight Asian teenagers carrying bags and wearing backpacks exited the station doors and came out to the bus waiting area where we were. They looked like a group of students who were together, and they saw Ben's sign first and came up to him. He read the verse on the sign to them, and he talked with them for a moment or two. They looked like they were in a hurry to catch their bus so after conversing with Ben they turned around and walked in my direction. They saw my sign and came walking in my direction. Apparently, Ben told them we both were Christians. When they came over, I asked them if they'd ever seen a sign like this. I knew that they were short on time and wouldn't have long to chat, so I quickly explained the three doors on my gospel sign. When I finished with the last door, they informed me

WHILE AT A TRAIN STATION

they all were Christians from South Korea, and they were here in the United States on a tour for two weeks. Since some people use the term "Christian" so loosely today I didn't want to assume that every person professing to be a Christian truly understands what it means, I asked them if they ever repented and put their trust in Jesus Christ alone for salvation. They informed me they did, but couldn't stay any longer and needed to board their bus that just arrived. But they were very encouraged and thanked us for being out in public for the cause of Jesus Christ and His gospel. I deflected all the glory to Him and then challenged them to be soul winners while they were here in the U.S. and when they returned to their country. Ben and I equipped them with gospel tracts and sent them on their way as they walked to their bus, looking back saying "God bless you" and "thank you." It was awesome to meet those Christians from South Korea, and who knows how God will use this encounter to stir a burning zeal in their hearts for the evangelization of the lost in their country. God is not looking for ability, but availability, and if Ben and I weren't available for God to use as soul winners that night, perhaps we might have never met and shared mutual encouragement with these Christians from across the sea. **PTL!**

> ***"Those who engage in the work of winning souls are rewarded by the deep sense of joy and satisfaction that comes to them."[7]***
>
> Francis Dixon

EVANGELISM'S FLIPSIDE

Later in the evening, a Brazilian man named Antonio approached us. He professed to be a Christian already, which is great. However, I still like to share the gospel with Christians to equip and encourage them to be soul winners if they aren't already. Hebrews 10:24 instructs Christians to "consider one another to provoke unto love and to good works." I can't think of any good work more loving than giving the gospel to the lost and inviting them to be born again. After Antonio read Ben's sign, his bus arrived. To our utter amazement, he was so interested in the subject of our conversation, he said, "My bus is here, but I will wait for the next one because I want to hear this." I then showed him three things God has never seen. As I was talking to Antonio, a middle-aged man named Peter came up on the right side of Ben to talk. Ben witnessed to him, and Peter said he was not ready to trust Christ just yet, but he was researching and willing to take gospel literature from Ben to take home and think about. As soon as Peter left, I finished up showing Antonio the gospel. He told Ben and I that he accepted Christ as his Saviour when he was seventeen years old and was now in his 40s. I asked him how his walk with God was going, and Antonio said he'd been walking with God ever since he got saved, but it was clear that Antonio was never challenged to be a soul winner. The first part of Proverbs 27:17 says, *"Iron sharpeneth iron."* As Christians, we should not only seek the salvation of the lost but also seek the sharpening of the saved regarding soul winning, which is the second most neglected part of the Christian life, behind prayer. Ben and I finished up our talk with Antonio, gave him some gospel tracts and a video on hell I produced, and exhorted him to find a solid Bible-believing, soul-winning church in his area that would train him to fulfill the Great Commission. **PTL!**

> *"My only joys therefore are that when God has given me a work to do, I have not refused it."[8]*
>
> C.T. Studd

After speaking with Antonio, just to my left was standing a young Spanish woman. I noticed her show up when we were chatting with Antonio. She had her ears plugged up with earphones and her face in her phone, which is typical of this generation. I'm even guilty of that myself sometimes, as it's just a sign of the technological times! Anyway, this woman was looking over towards the passenger drop off/pick up area of the station as if she was waiting for someone to arrive. She was physically attractive and because she was standing near our gospel signs and seemed to pull attention away from our signs; we thought it possible the Devil could have brought her over to be a distraction. So I left my approximately two feet long sign with Ben and walked a few steps over to her and asked if she spoke Spanish. She said she did. I then gave her a pocket-sized miniature Spanish Bible. She said she also read English as well and told me her name was Sandy. I asked Sandy if she ever saw people out here like Ben and me who (in the world's eyes) looked like fools for Jesus. To my surprise, she said she didn't think we looked like fools, and in fact, she said only narrow-minded people would think we were fools for being out here with our gospel signs trying to point people to Jesus!

Rather intrigued by this statement, I asked her "What is your religious background?" She told me her parents raised her Catholic, but she was not active in her faith. She also said she had a Seventh Day Adventist friend who tried to get her into that religion but she wasn't interested. So I asked Sandy if she believed in God and she said yes. Then I asked her, "Sandy what do you believe happens when you die?" She said she didn't know, but it concerned her. Then I asked, "Are you a good person?" Again she said yes. That's not a total shocker because the Bible says most people will proclaim their own goodness (Proverbs 20:6). I believe the reason people do this is that they don't understand just how sinful they really are in God's eyes and they *won't* understand until Christians faithfully hold up the mirror of God's Law so they can see how they don't measure up to His standard of righteousness. The Apostle Paul himself said, *"I had not known sin, but **by the law**: for I had not known lust, **except the law had said**, Thou shalt not covet"* (emphasis mine). Soul winners must not give in to the temptation to "get numbers" and therefore water down the gospel message by lessening the severity of sin. The lost must not see themselves as compared to other sinners. Instead, they must see themselves compared to God's perfect Law, so they will see their sin as *"exceedingly sinful"* (Rom 7:13) rather than just mere mistakes made by imperfect people.

After Sandy told me she believed she was a good person, I pulled out my pocket-sized New Testament (which every soul winner should own) and began at Romans 3:23. I showed her in the Bible what God says about sin, so she could see it for herself and know that I was not just giving my opinion. I asked her if she knew what the word *sin* meant. It's vitally important for soul winners to have a habit of asking the prospect questions like this along the way. This will help keep the prospect's mind focused on what we are discussing (namely the gospel) and also helps to keep our two-person dialogue from devolving into our one-person monologue. We want to lead and steer the conversation, but we shouldn't dominate it. So Sandy nodded her head confirming she knew what sin was and then I took her through a few of the Ten Commandments so she could know what sins she was personally guilty of. It was one thing for Sandy to believe that "all have sinned" against their Creator, but it's another to believe that she has *personally* sinned against God. When witnessing to the lost, soul winners must not make sin just a general concern but also a personal one. Sandy confessed to breaking at least three of the Ten Commandments I showed her. I then said, "Sandy, I'm not judging you, but upon your own admission of violating God's Law, on Judgment Day when God judges you by that Law what will you plead innocent or guilty?" She said she would be guilty, and then I asked if she'd go to heaven or end up in hell. I asked, "Does it concern you to know you are on your way to hell?" She said yes, but she believed that as long as she went to church and did good deeds she could make up for her sins. I then showed her verses like Ephesians 2:8-9 and Romans 6:23 explaining that salvation is a gift and there is *nothing* anyone could ever do to earn it. I explained to her she could not "make up" for her sins because she cannot travel back in time and undo the past. Besides this, our good works are not good at all in God's eyes.

As Bible teacher J. Vernon McGee once said: *"God accepts dirty sinners, not dirty laundry"* and according to God our good works are as dirty laundry (Isaiah 64:6). I took Sandy over to 1st John 1:7 and explained the good news that Jesus Christ came and died on the cross and His shed blood cleanses us from *all* of our sins. The word *all* means *all* and that's *all* that it means! I explained to Sandy that through the shed blood of the sinless Lord Jesus, all of a person's sins (past, present, and future) are forever washed away. Now you may think I spent hours sharing the gospel with her, but in fact, our conversation only took about five or six minutes. A gospel conversation should be thorough, but it does not and should not be too long. With the Lord's help, as you learn to stay on point and deliver the unfiltered gospel message, with practice you'll be able to do it in just a few short minutes.

So I then showed Sandy Romans 10:13 and told her it is not enough to just believe in Jesus with her head, but to be saved she needed to respond to the invitation to repent and put her trust in Jesus alone. Acts 20:21 states that the lost are called to *"repentance toward God, and faith toward our Lord Jesus Christ."* Thus the word, *repent* means "to turn toward one direction from the opposite direction."

Let me pause from my discussion with Sandy here to point something out. I don't believe biblical repentance means that a lost man must completely stop all sinning, clean up his life and be sinless *before* Christ can save him. If it was impossible for the Apostle Paul to refrain from all sin and be sinless as a man *already* saved (Rom 7:15-19), then it's likewise impossible for an unsaved man to do that. Besides, the Bible **nowhere** says the prerequisite for salvation is to stop all sinful behavior. That would be salvation by works and therefore a false gospel. Contrary to what some popular Christian leaders are teaching today, the *only* prerequisite for salvation is that a person truly turns to

God and trust in His Son Jesus as explained earlier in Acts 20:21. These Christian leaders are skewing the meaning of repentance and making repentance an outward change when repentance is first an *inward* change, a matter of the heart. As the verse above and similar verses show repentance and faith are two opposite sides of the same coin; you cannot have one without the other. When a person *truly* repents, their heart (the inward man) turns to and trusts in Christ and then eventually (as they mature spiritually) their behavior (outward man) will follow. We see this in 2nd Corinthians 3:15-16 in which Paul (referring to unsaved Jews) says, *"But even unto this day, when Moses is read, the vail is upon their heart. Nevertheless when it shall turn to the Lord, the vail shall be taken away."* Scripture here is teaching that until the Jewish people repent (turn to the Lord in their hearts), the veil will remain and they will remain blinded to their Messiah, the Lord Jesus Christ. It is clear the Bible teaches that repentance is a *change* in the heart, which results in a changed life. Though the change may happen at different times or at a different pace for different people a person who is genuinely repentant and converted *will* eventually show evidence of their conversion just as both John the Baptist and the Apostle Paul spoke about (Matt 3:8; Acts 26:20).

Now I'd like to bring up a very important issue as it relates to soul winning. There may come a point (while the soul winner shares the gospel with the prospect and he's ready to trust Christ as Savior) where the soul winner helps the prospect to pray what's known as a "Sinner's Prayer." I'm not totally against that idea. However, I don't consider it a mandatory method we must use at all times in all places no matter what. Nowhere does Scripture say an unsaved person must "*pray* to be saved." Pointing this out may ruffle feathers because unfortunately the "Sinner's Prayer" has become like a sacred cow to many soul winners and they use it religiously. Don't hate me because I'm telling the truth here. The Bible doesn't say "pray to the Lord Jesus Christ and thou shalt be saved" but *"**Believe** on the Lord Jesus Christ, and thou shalt be saved"* (emphasis mine).

Mark 16:16 teaches that a person is condemned not because they didn't *pray*, (or get baptized, etc.) but because they didn't *believe*. Faith in Christ is what is required for salvation, not a prayer, baptism or anything else. As a former Catholic myself, I must warn soul winners to be very careful to not lead people (especially from pagan religions like Hinduism and Catholicism who already have a ritualistic tradition of praying repetitious mantras) to believe that praying a prayer will save them. Praying a scripted prayer is not what saves them, but faith in Christ saves them.

EVANGELISM'S FLIPSIDE

Many Christians who believe the "Sinner's Prayer" approach must apply to every person at all times like to passages like Romans 10:13 or Revelation 3:20 to justify this practice, but sadly they have to *misuse* and thus misapply such passages to do so. The context of those passages is not at all talking about lost people being required to pray a scripted "Sinner Prayer" formula or "ask Jesus into their heart" to get saved. Bible teachers who are way more knowledgeable in the Scriptures than I have pointed out that Romans 9 deals with the *past* spiritual condition of Israel and Romans 11 deals with the *future* spiritual condition of Israel (the true remnant of those who God foreknew would get saved). Romans chapter 10 is about the present-day spiritual condition of those out of Israel who hear the gospel. Specifically, the thought behind Romans 10:13 comes from the Old Testament book of Joel concerning the unfolding events outlined in the beginning verses of Joel 2. It has special reference to Christ's Second Advent where (considering the impending judgment to come on the world) salvation will be granted to "whosoever" (both Jews *and* Gentiles) that turn to Christ in faith instead of fight against Him (as the rest of the world will do when He returns) and be condemned. It is not saying that salvation is only for those who verbally and audibly call on the Lord because that would exclude those who (for various biological or medical reasons) can't speak. Instead, the main point the Holy Spirit (through Paul) wants us to understand is that the Gentiles or Jews whose *hearts* turn to the Lord in faith will be saved. It is that simple.

Romans 10:9-13 is a call for those Israelis who truly believe on Jesus as Messiah for salvation to publicly confess and display their faith, unlike those who (because of fear) weren't willing to make their faith in Jesus public (John 12:42-43). Here in Romans 10, Paul is admonishing Israelis to get saved and to be more concerned with the praise of God than with the praise of men. So while Romans 10:13 admonishes the Israelites to "call upon the name of the Lord," it is not saying they or anyone else must recite some scripted prayer phrase by phrase as a requirement for salvation.

Then in Revelation 3:20, Jesus is not knocking at the door of a sinner's heart waiting for them to invite Him in. Rather, He's symbolically standing outside the church of Laodicea. The church (as a whole) had apparently gotten to the place where they had no time for Jesus and had shut Him out, and so He was knocking at the door seeking for them to allow Him back in. In Revelation 3:20, Jesus is specifically seeking the fellowship of the saints, not the salvation of sinners. Therefore, it's a misuse of Scripture to isolate this verse and claim it's about sinners asking Jesus into their hearts.

As soul winners, we do not have to give a lost person a scripted apology to read. We don't have to tell them what to say. For example, if a married man, having come under deep conviction and godly sorrow, now realizes just how bad he has offended his wife and deeply hurt her, and seeks her forgiveness, he will know what to say. He will admit his fault and will humbly ask for her forgiveness. He will say it in his own words, from the sincerity of a repentant and contrite heart. He will not need a pre-made apology to read; especially when written by a complete stranger, he's just met! I hope you understand my point here. I cannot stress it enough. If you have explained the gospel to the prospect and they are ready to get saved, then invite them to tell God (in their own words) they admit their guilt, and want Him to forgive them and save them. So again, if an unsaved person has heard the gospel, is being convicted by the Holy Spirit and wants salvation, we (as soul winners) will not need to give them what to say to God word for word.

A lost person must first be ready to trust Christ. If they're not ready, then don't pressure them to the "Sinner's Prayer" anyway. We must invite sinners to trust Christ, but we must not coerce them into it. In fact, it's better if you let them pray in their own words (as that's more heartfelt and real) rather than you telling them word for word what to say. If they're under conviction by the Holy Spirit, and their heart is contrite and repentant then He'll help verbalize a genuine confession of faith. If they've never prayed before and really don't know where to begin, then perhaps (as a helpful example) you could show them David's prayer (Psalm 51), the publican's prayer (Luke 18:13) or a prayer outline used at the end of the tracts offered at EvanTell.org. I don't believe in pressuring or manipulating anyone to pray a "Sinner's Prayer" just for the sake of getting them to say it. Unfortunately, this can and has led to false conversions. It also gives people false assurances and has had disastrous consequences for the cause of Christ. And let's remember that a person can pray a "Sinner's Prayer" all day long, but unless their heart is truly repentant, they will not get saved. It doesn't matter as much what a person's mouth is doing, God cares more about what their heart is doing (Matt 15:8). Although generally, I'm not against a "Sinner's Prayer", I still think it's important for soul winners to push for true repentance in the heart, not a mere mental assent through the repeating a scripted prayer.

After asking Sandy if this gospel message I was delivering to her made sense, she said it did. Then I gave her a recap and reminded her that there were two things that had to take place in order for God to save her and they were: 1) she had to repent and 2) she had to put her trust in Jesus alone. Then I asked, "What would prevent you from making peace with God and asking Jesus from your heart to save you right now?" Sandy paused, and then said, "I don't know." I asked,

"Is there something in your life or perhaps some sin hindering you from accepting Jesus Christ as your Saviour?" She put her head down and then said, "Maybe." Then I told Sandy that no sin is worth going to hell for, and I pleaded with her to think about her eternal destiny because tomorrow is guaranteed for nobody. I assured her I wasn't trying to use scare tactics, but in fact, I genuinely cared where she would spend eternity and this is the reason I was out there soul winning that night. Well, the person she was waiting for showed up and she walked towards that direction. As Sandy was going, I gave her a video I've produced on the reality of a literal place called hell, and also some gospel tracts, and asked Sandy to look at the material and begged her not to take the risk of dying without Christ. She thanked me for the material and she gave me her word she would look at it and consider what I talked to her about. For me, it was joy unspeakable to have the privilege of planting the gospel seed, and parting ways on good terms for another soul winner to water that seed so that perhaps one day soon God adds her to the Kingdom. **PTL!**

> *"It is the only happy life to live for the salvation of souls."[9]*
>
> D.L. Moody

Since Sandy and I finished talking, I walked back to get the gospel sign and rejoined Ben. At this point in the evening, we had been out witnessing for several hours,

WHILE AT A TRAIN STATION

and now it was dark outside and the temperature had dropped significantly since we had arrived at this train station. And in reaction to the cold air, my nose ran, so I needed to reach into my pocket and pull out a tissue to wipe it. To free my hands to get the tissue, I laid the sign down flat over this ledge to the left of the stairwell that led to the lower level bus area. Within a minute or two a college-aged man named Aziz approaches us. He walked right over to the sign as it lay flat and read it. In Acts 8:30 when Philip the evangelist saw the Ethiopian eunuch reading the scroll of Isaiah, he asked, *"Understandest thou what thou readest?"* This is what I asked Aziz, except in the modern vernacular. He was so enthralled in what he was reading he didn't respond. So I waited a few more moments and then asked again, "Do you understand what you're reading?" Again Aziz didn't answer. Then he looked up at me with a puzzled look on his face. "Have you ever seen something like this before?" I asked. He shook his head to signal that he had not. Then I explained the verses on the sign to him one door at a time. He admitted that the "all" of Romans 3:23 included him, that he was a sinner too. Once I finished the last door, Aziz asked me "What do you mean by 'saved'? What are you saved from?" I said, "That's a great question." I then explained to Aziz that because he has sinned, God is holy and will punish sin. I then took him to Revelation 21:8 which says, "But the fearful, and unbelieving, and the abominable, and murderers, and whoremongers, and sorcerers, and idolaters, and all liars, shall have their part in the lake which burneth with fire and brimstone: which is the second death." Ben stepped into the conversation and we explained to Aziz that he broke God's Law and Jesus paid his fine when He went to the cross.

At this moment Aziz said he had to get going, and Ben then reached over to give him a gospel tract which had a picture of three crosses on the front and had the words Paid In Full on the front. As soon as Aziz saw the tract, he put his hand up to refuse the tract and said, "I am a Muslim." I then encouraged Aziz to put his trust in the Saviour, not to trust in his religious affiliation because he knows he already admitted to being a sinner and a holy God will punish sin in the Lake of Fire, no matter what his religious label is. I even offered him a video I produced on how science supports the Bible's claim of the literal existence of the lake of fire mentioned in the book of Revelation. We pleaded with him to reconsider. He first took the DVD and then slowly and reluctantly he took the Paid in Full gospel tract. "Thank you," said Aziz, much to our surprise, and then off he went. **PTL!**

> *"I cannot tell you what joy it gave me to bring the first soul to the Lord Jesus Christ. I have tasted almost all the pleasures that this world can give. I do not suppose there is one that I have not experienced, but I can tell you that those pleasures were as nothing compared to the joy that the saving of that one soul gave me."[10]*
>
> C.T. Studd

WHILE AT A TRAIN STATION

At this point in the evening, there were still many people standing around waiting for their transportation to arrive, and not wanting any dead time in between prospects, I remained proactive. I saw a tall man wearing big headphones look my direction, so I waved him over to us. I asked him if he ever saw this sign before. His name was Francisco, and he was from Angola. It's always exciting when you obey the Lord and talk with lost people because you never know whom He will bring your way and what part of the world they'll be from! Francisco and I made some small talk for, and I found out he was in college and perhaps at that moment was pondering his future. As soul winners it is a good idea to be folksy and begin a conversation by briefly talking about the natural realm (such as the weather, sports, any relevant news.) before you get into the supernatural realm because that's' what Jesus did with the Samaritan woman at the well (John 4:7). And since Jesus was the Master soul winner, shouldn't we want to do as Jesus did? I asked Francisco what he was studying in college. After he told me, I asked him, "If you died unexpectedly do you know where you would spend eternity?" He looked at me rather stunned and puzzled, but then he said: "You know, no I don't know." "This is why we are out here," I told him. Then we discussed the gospel as outlined on the sign I was holding. He had no questions for me the entire time I was explaining the gospel, as he seemed to soak it up, but it was hard not to notice the frozen look on his face. So I asked, "Has anyone ever told what I told you" and sadly he said nobody had. It's hard to fathom, but unfortunately, there are people in America (many who have been in the country for years) that still have not had Christians care enough about their soul to engage them in a gospel conversation. In 1st Corinthians 15:34 Scripture calls followers of Christ to *"Awake to righteousness, and sin not; for some have not the knowledge of God: I speak this **to your shame**"* (emphasis mine).

When Christians talk about the "mission field," we shouldn't only refer to foreign missions because, in reality, the Great Commission is more about people than it is about geography. And while there *may* be more of a need for the gospel in foreign lands who haven't had the same opportunities, the United States is still a mission field and a big one at that! Some parts of America may be gospel hardened, but by and large, America is more gospel ignorant than anything else. Why? Because we have so many false teachers preaching false gospels (under various religious labels) that there is much confusion in our land and therefore much ignorance of the true gospel. Truly *"the labourers are few"* (Matt 9:37) as it seems like there are more false teachers out there spreading their perversions of the truth than there are true gospel preachers. So Christians who are not obeying the Lord regarding evangelism are part of this problem, not part of the solution!

After explaining the gospel to Francisco I told him what God has done in my life since my salvation. He was listening intently, and at just that moment his bus had arrived and he informed me he had to get going. But before he left, I asked, "So Francisco, since you know how simple God has made it for you to be saved, what would stop you from putting your trust in Jesus for His gift of salvation tonight?" He said he didn't know, but said he'd like to look into it more. Then I gave him a gospel tract and a copy of my DVD on hell and urged him to take this seriously as this was about his eternal destiny. "Thank you, I will," he said. As he went I assured him, I would pray for him and while expressing his appreciation he went towards his bus. **PTL!**

> *"To serve the devil, even when he gives us most of the sweets of sin, is intolerable bondage to a sensible, awakened sinner; but to serve Christ, how pleasant, how joyful!"*[11]
>
> Charles H. Spurgeon

By now the foot traffic in and out of the bus entrance to the station had dwindled and my soul winning partner and I had been out witnessing for several hours. It was getting late in the evening, so we packed up and head towards Ben's car which was parked around the corner from the train station. Ben was carrying his sign in such a way that the words of the sign were facing outward towards the few remaining people in front of the station. As we were walking, a young Ethiopian woman came up to us and said, "Are you taking prayer requests"? The blue words "Need prayer?" on Ben's sign had apparently drawn her to us. "Yes, of course," said Ben. She told us her name was Josie. She was a youth outreach worker in her church and wanted us to pray for the best way to conduct teen outreach. I then asked her about her relationship with the Lord. "I grew up Christian," she said. I get a little concerned when people tell me that because many people think they're Christian just because they grew up with Christian parents. According to Scripture *nobody* is born a Christian or "grows up Christian." She then explained how when she was younger, she came to make a personal decision to trust Christ as her Saviour, and I breathed a sigh of relief after she said that. Convinced that Josie's salvation testimony was genuine, I then asked her if she knew how to give the gospel to the lost and lead someone to Christ. The reason I asked her that was because if she didn't know how to effectively explain the gospel herself, she may have a hard time having an effective outreach ministry to teenagers, children, and adults. I was sensitive to the fact that Josie was waiting for her bus to arrive, so I quickly but thoroughly explained how she could use the Bible verses as seen on my sign to lead a person to Christ. After I finished, Ben opened his pocket New Testament to Acts 8:26, and there they looked at Philip the evangelist as a good example.

God used him to lead the Ethiopian eunuch to Jesus because Philip, rather than go in his own power, was willing to be filled with the power of the Holy Spirit (Acts 8:26, 29). We then gave Josie a stack of our gospel tracts and emphasized the importance of also having a pocket-sized New Testament on hand. This is essential if we want to be ready for the "eunuchs" God leads us to like He did with Philip. Now, you can obviously still witness to an unsaved person even if you don't have those tools with you, but isn't it better to be equipped than not? Just as Josie's bus was pulling up to the station, she wanted us to pray for her. Then Ben led all three of us in a quick prayer for Josie, and for God to give her and her church leaders a passion for souls and wisdom for her teen outreach project. She showered us with "thank you" for encouraging her and we thanked her for likewise encouraging us because none of us is an island (Rom 14:7). As Christians, whether we live or we die, we're all accountable to God. Considering this truth, in evangelism, we will either work to encourage or discourage others in this area of Christian life. There is absolutely no middle road. When we as Christians decide to be soul winners, not only are we going to please God by our obedience, we will also be an encouragement to other believers we find along our travels. The Bible says for Christians to *"... seek that ye may excel to the edifying of the church"* (1 Cor 14:12). In these spiritually dark times we live in, we need to find even more ways of edifying one another and one great way to do that is by going out into the world and seeking the salvation of souls for the Lord Jesus. **PTL!**

> **"The men who are putting everything into Christ's undertaking are getting out of life its sweetest and most precious rewards."[12]**
>
> J. Campbell White

After thanking the Lord for meeting Josie and bidding her farewell, Ben and I were hungry and headed to Harvard Square in Cambridge, the next town over from Somerville, for a bite to eat. We got there and went into a Japanese-style franchise restaurant which I'm familiar with because I go to their Boston location as much as I can. When we arrived the place wasn't too busy with customers, probably because it was after 8 pm. After we ordered, we prayed and thanked the Lord for providing our food and we enjoyed our fellowship as we recalled what God had done that evening. Feeling generous, Ben decided that he would pay for my meal, which was an added blessing because nothing beats delicious healthy food other than when it's free! After we ate and had fellowship, Ben had to take a call on his phone from his brother.

Up to this point, I didn't talk to our waitress that much. But since he was on the phone and the place wasn't too busy, I found out how our waitress was doing spiritually. She was a young woman, and I found out her name was Edith. I explained to Edith what Ben, and I had been doing prior to coming to the restaurant. I told her about the "three things God hasn't seen" sign I had been speaking to people about. I told her how we're living in spiritually dark times and God has impressed upon me the urgency of the hour, to not slack in getting the gospel to "whosoever will." To my surprise, Edith said, "I agree, America used to be on fire for God and now she's moving away from God, and it's very sad." Sensing an open door to shift the conversation from America's relationship with God to her personal relationship with Him, I said, "Edith let me ask you this: do you know what it means to be saved? God forbid if you die tonight, do you know where you would spend your eternity?" To that, she replied, "Oh yes, I believe in Jesus, I'm Catholic." Now, I'm thinking she may truly be a Christian, but there's also a chance she doesn't really understand salvation either and just believes herself saved because of her "Catholic" label. So, not wanting to take a chance she isn't really saved, I asked her if I could take a moment and give her my testimony as a former Catholic myself.

In Matthew 10:16 Jesus told His disciples "Behold, I send you forth as sheep in the midst of wolves: be ye therefore wise as serpents, and harmless as doves," (emphasis mine). Now, if you're at a restaurant and you want to explain the gospel to your waiter or waitress, it is wise to first ask their permission. This way you don't get them in trouble with their boss for taking up their work time. Being tactful like this will help you avoid unnecessarily offending them and potentially losing the opportunity for yourself or another soul winner to witness to them in the future. So Edith agreed to let me take a few moments to talk with her about her soul. I briefly gave her my testimony on how I was raised in a Catholic context, but wasn't saved and had no assurance of going to heaven, until someone cared enough to show me from the Bible how I could know for sure of going to heaven. She then broke in at this point and told me she had put her trust in Jesus for salvation when she was a little child, around seven years old. I asked, "So you are sure you depend on Jesus Christ and His death and resurrection alone for your salvation?" She assured me she did. "You do not trust Mary or the church to save you, but Jesus Christ alone, right?" Again she said yes. I wanted to make sure she had biblical salvation. I then told her that since my salvation and departure from Catholicism, I attend a church where people are taught from an open Bible, and encouraged her to do the same. "Oh, my church has Bible studies. Though they didn't before, but the Catholic Church has been changing," Edith said. The Bible in Jeremiah 13:23 asked a rhetorical question, "Can the Ethiopian change his skin, or the leopard his spots?" The answer is no. Is the Catholic Church changing to become more biblical? Maybe on the surface it is, but the foundation of Catholicism is still unbiblical to the core and any student of the Bible knows this. Upon hearing Edith's response I resisted the temptation to give her a sermon on the unbiblical teachings and practices of Catholicism because I didn't want to seem like I was bashing her church. This would have unnecessarily turned her off. I don't doubt that there are Catholics who have genuinely been saved, but this is despite what Catholicism teaches and not because of it. We had talked for several minutes and I asked her if I could leave some material with her, along with the address to a more biblical church for her to look into further, and she agreed. After paying, Ben and I got up to leave and Edith expressed her thanks for caring enough to talk with her about the things of God. And who knows, as Edith continues to study the Bible, she may realize that Catholicism isn't biblical after all and the door will be open for her God to lead her to a biblical church. **PTL!**

A Strange Encounter

"The out-and-out Christian is a joyful Christian."[13]

Alexander Maclaren

One night late in January, I was doing open-air preaching in downtown Boston on the Commons. I had two other Christians with me who were passing out gospel tracts as I was speaking through my hands-free mini voice amplifier. I was preaching about the Bible's description of the second death, namely the literal place the Bible calls the lake of fire. After a while of being out there preaching, a woman (whom I originally mistook for a man) came along and heckled us. She didn't directly heckle me and try to stop my preaching, but she took turns heckling each of the other Christian men with me that night. These two Christian men were zealous for the Lord, but they were relatively new at soul winning, and this woman, who was probably within our age range, was successfully getting them off track and down rabbit trails. The goal of soul winning, just like that of a mailman, is to deliver the message, but this woman was asking all these questions and making incoherent statements. It was hard to tell if she was really interested in the gospel or if she was a demon-possessed tool of Satan to stop the men from giving out the gospel tracts. I preached for about ten minutes, and when I finished, she was still there heckling one of the Christian men. So I walked over there and began a conversation with her. I learned that her name was Riah. With a smile on her face and giggling she was making statements like "I wrote the Bible" and "I've read the Jewish Hindu Koran" and so forth. It was hard to tell if she was mentally unbalanced or demon possessed. But she apparently had no fear of the God her mouth was blaspheming. So I pulled out the Sword of the Spirit (my pocket New Testament) and I showed her what the Bible says about sin and the Holiness of God. Immediately her mouth closed, and she became quiet and attentive. It was amazing!

Romans 3:19 says, *"Now we know that what things soever the law saith, it saith to them who are under the law: that every mouth may be stopped, and all the world may become guilty before God."* Soul winners must be careful to not gloss over the Law when speaking to the lost because as Psalm 19:7 says, *"the Law of the LORD is perfect, converting the soul."* The Law also works as a schoolmaster that brings people to Jesus and helps them to see why they need Him as Saviour (Gal 3:24). When God's Law is correctly used by the soul winner (1 Tim 1:8) one of two things will result. It will either convict people and lead them to repentance, or they will harden their hearts and stop their ears just as the Jewish leaders did with Stephen's message (Acts 7:57).

When Riah tried to get me off track, I would keep pointing back to the Scriptures and showing her "it is written..., it is written..., it is written..." I learned from the best as Jesus used this same tactic with the Devil (Matt 4:4-11). After thoroughly explaining sin and its penalty, I also showed Riah that the *"... gift of God is eternal life through Jesus Christ our Lord"* (Rom 6:23). I explained to her how she must repent and trust Jesus Christ as her Saviour and Lord to receive eternal life. She didn't want to hear anymore and said she had to get going. But as she was leaving, she took a Chick tract I extended to her and even muttered a soft "thank you" as she turned and walk away. That was one of the strangest yet exciting encounters I've experienced while out fishing for souls. But I know this if the gospel is powerful enough to change a demon-possessed man named Legion (Luke 8:35) it can change anyone no matter how strange they may appear. Therefore, no matter to whom I give the gospel or where I am giving it, God always makes it an adventure by the people He leads me to. **PTL!**

Logan Airport

"Expect great things from God; attempt great things for God"[14]

William Carey

One Saturday morning in September I was at Logan International Airport in Boston, Massachusetts because I was heading to the Central American country of Belize for a mission trip. The previous evening I was in a mission conference, and it was there in prayer I asked the Lord if He would prevent me from returning home from Belize *until* I gave out all four hundred gospel tracts I was taking with me on the trip. I did not want to come back home from the mission trip until I could give them all away. Missions are about people and I wanted to accomplish my goal for the cause of the Great Commission before I came back to the States. Before I could board my plane, I had to go through the Transportation Security Administration (TSA) security checkpoint line like everyone else. Since I would be at an airport, I thought it would be appropriate to bring some *Flight 144* Chick tracts with me.

I pulled out the tracts and offered them to people in line with me. I also handed tracts to the TSA agents who, although they may have the most annoying job in the world, they still need Jesus too! So as soon as I passed through the x-ray machine, I handed the first TSA agent I saw a Chick tract. The man accepted it and looked at the tract and asked: "What's this about?" I replied, "Sir, it's a gospel tract that has a good message in it about how to know for sure you're on the way to heaven." In response, the man laughingly said: "I know I'm far from God, that's for sure." I replied "You don't have to be because He's' not far from you. Maybe God sent me to give that tract to you today to show you He wants you back." He said, "Thanks, you just might be right about that." **PTL!**

> *"Shall he (the Christian) not feel it to be his greatest glory to serve his God? And will there not be from this a stream of joy flowing over all our holy work?"[15]*
>
> Charles H. Spurgeon

I then handed a *Flight 144* Chick tract to the next TSA agent that was standing to the right of this man. He took it and he pulled me off to the side to chat a moment. At first, I thought I was in trouble or that he would scold me for passing these tracts out. No such a thing happened, but he expressed his thanks instead. His name was Marcus, and he said, referring to the first TSA agent, "Thank you for giving him a tract, as I've also been witnessing to him for a while now." Wow, what a pleasant surprise! As we were talking, we noticed two Brazilian women coming through the TSA x-ray checkpoint wearing the same bright yellow T-shirts which had a date and time on it for some event. I made a comment to Marcus that the women looked like they were going to a conference and he confirmed that they were because one of the women was his wife and the other was her friend. He told me they were both Christians, and they were going to a Christian women's conference in Florida. Just then I realized that Marcus pulled me off to the side not only to encourage me for giving out tracts, but I learned that he wanted me to meet his wife and give her and her friend some gospel tracts to take with them. I greeted Marcus' wife and her friend and briefly explained my testimony and that I was on my way to Belize for a mission trip. Then Marcus told me it was his wife, who got saved first, and then he got saved about six months ago (from that day we were talking there together) and that God had given him a burden for his fellow TSA co-workers. He then asked me to give him more of the *Flight 144* Chick tracts. Some other TSA agents standing nearby didn't take a tract. But as I headed to my boarding gate, Marcus said he was encouraged by the zeal God has given me for the lost. But I assured Marcus that it was he who had really encouraged me because he actively witnesses to his TSA coworkers.

In this Laodicean church age, it seems like many Christians are just too full of the cares of this world to be hot for evangelism (Mark 4:9). However, just as the coming of Stephanas, Fortunatus and Achaicus had refreshed Paul's spirit (1st Cor 16:17-18) it is always refreshing to my spirit to meet other Christians (outside my circle) who have not bowed the knee to the god of lukewarmness. I wished Marcus and the women Godspeed as I went on to the gate where my flight would leave from. **PTL!**

> **"Nothing can wholly satisfy the life of Christ within His followers except the adoption of Christ's purpose toward the world He came to redeem."[16]**
>
> J. Campbell White

I got to my gate and realized I still had plenty of time before I had to board the plane. I set my carry-on luggage down on one of the seats in front of the ticket counter where my gate was. It was around 9:30 in the morning and from what I could see, most people were walking around or shopping around. I was still pretty tired from the night before because for some reason I don't sleep well the night before a flight. And on top of this, I am also not typically a morning person. I'm usually a night owl. So I sat there for a moment. I had a choice to make. I could either take a nap before the flight, I could check my email via the airport's Wi-Fi connection, or I could read something. Though I was pretty tired and in the flesh I didn't want to get up, none of those options were appealing. I couldn't stay there because just like Jeremiah (Jer 20:9) I had this burning desire in my bones to preach the Word! As someone once said, "The gospel is only good news if it gets there in time." I'm not sure who said it but I was thinking about that statement and I had all these gospel tracts on hand, and they wouldn't do any good staying in my pockets. So I got up and walked around giving out the *Flight 144* Chick tracts. As I was walking the corridors of Logan airport, I came to a store that sold cell phones and accessories. The only one in the store at the time was an employee. He was a young Asian man in his early 20s named Kevin. I said hello and made some small talk for a few minutes to be folksy and break the ice. It's very important that you build rapport with the people you want to give the gospel to. By eating with sinners I believe Jesus Himself built rapport with those He wanted to see saved (Mark 2:16-17). So after talking to him about things in the natural realm I transitioned into the spiritual.

"Kevin, let me ask you this," I said. "What do you believe happens when someone dies?" He wasn't sure what he believed about the afterlife or God, but he admitted he was leaning toward a belief in the theory of evolution. I shared with him what the Scriptures say. For someone who said he was not actively searching, Kevin still had a lot of questions for me. This was a good problem to have for it is always better for your prospect to be interested enough to ask questions rather than not be willing to have a conversation at all. Kevin wanted to know *why* I believed what I said I believed. You will meet people like Kevin who have sincere questions, therefore, God admonishes Christians to *"... be ready always to give an answer to every man that asketh you a reason of the hope that is in you with meekness and fear"* (1ˢᵗ Peter 3:15).

This does not mean that you must have all the answers to everyone who has a question. But it means that you could at least share your testimony with people and explain why you yourself came to believe the gospel and what Jesus has done in your life.

I first gave my testimony to Kevin and then showed Him in the Bible how he could receive the eternal life I've received through Christ. As we were talking people would come into the store, I'd pause and let him attend to the customers and then he'd let me continue showing him what God's Word says. We had a nice redemptive conversation with a good back-and-forth exchange of questions and answers, which is healthy. This is what should happen because again, presenting the gospel is more of a conversation than a one-man monologue presentation. We talked for about thirty minutes in between customers and then I had to head back over to the gate as they were making the announcements over the PA system that boarding was about to start. During the conversation, Kevin told me he had a daughter and that he was trying to be a good father by providing what she needs. I told him: "I'm glad to hear that, but don't you think it is also important that your daughter grows up knowing the truth about where she came from? You don't want her to grow up believing the lie of evolution, do you?" I do not know Kevin's motivations for believing in that, so I do not want to judge his heart, but most people hold on to a lie like that for moral reasons, not for intellectual ones.

Many people cling to the theory of evolution since they believe it'll help them escape being accountable to a Creator. Evolution is the intellectual drug of choice for people who do not want to be morally accountable to the Creator. I didn't judge Kevin's heart, but I gave him the benefit of the doubt he really had sincere questions hindering him from accepting what the Bible says. So I went back to my luggage and got Kevin a DVD on the truth about creation produced by Dr Kent Hovind. Before I left to board my plane, I asked Kevin if I could pray with him. "Sure, I would appreciate that," he said, so right in front of the store with people walking by us, I prayed and asked God to open Kevin's eyes to the truth. I prayed that Kevin would be humble enough to accept it, repent and get saved and then share this truth with his daughter so she could grow up knowing the truth too. He extended his hand to shake mine and expressed his gratitude. I then thanked him as well for giving me his time. Kevin made it clear he wasn't ready to turn to Christ right there in the store. But, have faith, my beloved! Who knows what will happen! It's exciting to imagine what the Word of God will accomplish when someone has planted the gospel seed! I know one thing, it won't return void (Isa 55:11). **PTL!**

In the Air

"As for the true Believer in Jesus, he serves his God because he loves to serve Him...To him it is the greatest of all earthly joys, and a foretaste of joys celestial to serve the Lord with hands, and heart, and strength, and to spend and be spent for His glory."[17]

Charles H. Spurgeon

On the first of two flights I'd be on in the day en route to Belize, I met Rudy. I chatted with him about the natural and then swung into the supernatural. He told me he got saved when he was 6yrs old. Rudy told me he also has a son named Ricardo (19), and a daughter Tracy (21). He was distraught over the spiritual condition of his family. He told me Ricardo was not interested in anything that has to do with God at this point in his life and his daughter Tracy was a member of the JWs. When I was convinced that Rudy understood biblical salvation and that he was saved man, I asked him if he knew how to use the Bible and show someone else how to get saved. "Rudy, let me ask you something," I said. "If I was your best friend, and I was dying in the hospital and you're the only Christian I knew, and fearing that I might die soon, I asked you to come to the hospital and show me in the Bible how to get saved, would you know how?" Rudy admitted that he did not know how to do that. As Christians, it is *very* important that we learn how to use God's Word for the map to eternal life it is. Hebrew 4:12 says, *"For the word of God is quick, and powerful, and sharper than any twoedged sword, piercing even to the dividing asunder of soul and spirit, and of the joints and marrow, and is a discerner of the thoughts and intents of the heart."* The Apostle Peter said people are *"born again, not of corruptible seed, but of incorruptible, by the word of God, which liveth and abideth for ever"* (1st Pet 1:23). Ultimately, it is not what we say *about* the Word of God, but what the Word of God *itself* says. It can convert a soul because it alone is living and powerful.

Since all of God's Word is quick and powerful, there isn't just one set of verses or one way to show people from the Bible how to get saved. We can use any verse to lead people to salvation, such as John 3:16 or even Habakkuk 2:4 in the Old Testament, which God used to convert the famous Martin Luther. But depending on who you are talking to some passages of Scripture may be more effective than others. Many soul winners today use the passages that comprise the "Romans Road." These passages are a quick yet effective way to explain to someone what biblical salvation entails. On the way to Florida, there was an empty seat in between us and I used that the seat tray table to open my pocket-sized New Testament and teach Rudy the "Romans Road." It was exciting and encouraging to witness just how eager Rudy was to travel down this "road" with me. He broke out a pen and a piece of paper and jotted down the verses, and he said he would show them to his son and to his daughter at the next opportunity. I also encouraged him to invest in a pocket-sized New Testament because the flesh is weak and the more convenient it is to carry our Bible; the more likely we will have it with us when the need to use the Sword arises.

Our plane landed at Miami airport, and before going our separate ways we prayed together. Then what happened was completely of the Lord. Earlier in the day, while on the plane, I told Rudy that I requested that the Lord not allow me to return home until I reached my goal of giving away all my tracts. So just after we prayed and were about to part ways, and without me even asking, Rudy felt led to help me reach my goal. Upon extending his hand, I gave him several stacks of the *Flight 144* Chick tracts and both of us went our way rejoicing. **PTL!**

Miami Airport

"There is no joy outside of knowing Jesus and serving him."[18]

Karen Watson

While at Miami international airport, I had some time to kill, and although I was still pretty tired from a lack of sound sleep the night before, I was still fired up for God! I went walking around the airport passing out tracts on my way to the gate where I would board my flight to Belize. I noticed a group of women sitting together with several men. The women were wearing purple shirts that said "Women of Purpose" on the front and 1st John 3:8 from the Bible on the back. Needing to satisfy my curiosity, I walked over to them, and after handing each of them a *Flight 144* tract I soon discovered that they were professing Christians. They identified themselves as Pentecostal and they were heading to an evangelistic meeting in Belize. After giving them my testimony and talking with them for a while, they expressed interest in the Chick tracts I had and asked for some of the tracts so that they could also share in the joy and blessing of giving them out. Again, this was the Lord working, because not only did I not ask them to help me give the tracts away, but neither did I tell them I had a goal to give out all my tracts before returning home. In addition to this they already had some of their own tracts with them, but apparently liked my tracts more! Do you not see how my Lord was

EVANGELISM'S FLIPSIDE

working to help me reach my goal by raising up these Christians to assist me in distributing my tracts? What an amazingly gracious and kind Saviour, my Lord Jesus Christ is! That day was truly an exciting one, but in truth, there's always an adventure when Christians step out in faith and obedience to reach the lost as Jesus did. **PTL!**

Belize!

"The prospects are as bright as the promises of God."[19]

Adoniram Judson

It was a Saturday afternoon when I landed in Belize. The pastor and his family whom I came to serve with met me at the airport. On a Wednesday morning there, I loaded up my backpack and ventured out into the downtown area of Belize City. I spent several hours giving out my gospel tracts to those on the move and witnessing to people who would stop and talk. I also was handing out the pastor's church tracts along with their John and Romans booklets. Kayla, a young Belizean woman and faithful member of that church I was serving, owned a small restaurant in a busy intersection of downtown Belize, in the immediate area where I had been witnessing. After spending several hours emptying my backpack of gospel tracts in downtown Belize City, I headed over to Kayla's restaurant for a bite to eat and some much-needed shade, as it had been hot and sunny all that day. When I arrived she asked me to witness to her employees named Vanessa and Sylvia. Vanessa didn't claim to be a Christian. Sylvia is a professing Christian, but didn't go to church at all because she didn't want to have trouble with Roberto, her unsaved Catholic husband. Sylvia and Vanessa worked in the kitchen as cooks. So I went to the back, in the kitchen area and explain the gospel to them. Kayla was working the front counter area, and in between customers she would come back to the kitchen area and encourage her employees to heed the truth from God's Word I was sharing with them. At this point, a reader might think, "But why did you witness to Sylvia when she said she was already saved?" I mainly gave the gospel to Vanessa her non-Christian coworker. However, as I was doing it, I was showing Sylvia the Scripture verses I was using, not so she could get saved again (as that's unnecessary), but to equip and then challenge her to show the same thing to her husband at home hoping he too might get saved. Sylvia may be the only Christian her husband knows. I wanted to help sharpen her in soul winning because knowing the gospel is one thing, but being able and willing to use the Bible to explain it to lost people is quite another thing.

After I finished, Kayla asked me to lead them all in prayer right there in the kitchen area. Besides being filled with the joy of the Lord for having an opportunity to minister God's Word, Kayla knew that I had eaten nothing all afternoon, and (without me asking) God led Kayla to provide me with a full-sized plate of food, including a salad and drink at no cost. This was like having my favorite cake with a cherry on top. What an extra blessing for sure. **PTL!**

"It pays to serve Jesus ev'ry day,
It pays ev'ry step of the way;

BELIZE!

*Though the path way to Glory may
sometimes be drear,
You'll be happy each step of the way.*"[20]

Frank C. Huston

I was out in the hot sun for several hours giving out gospel tracts in downtown Belize City and after getting a tan I didn't need (because if you know me; you know I was already born with one!), and (as I mentioned previously), Kayla graciously provided me with a free meal and some much-needed shade at her restaurant. After some cool-down time, I still had a few more of my gospel tracts and gospel packets from the local church I was serving with that I wanted to give out. Now Kayla displayed some of her church tracts in a pile near the register at the takeout window, and besides this, she encouraged me to give the gospel packets to her customers while they were walking by or waiting in line. While I was standing in front of her restaurant, giving out the gospel packets, two young boys who were just released from school for the day, came up to the window and wanted to order some French fries. Kayla informed them they were short fifty cents. I was standing off to the side, and they approached me saying, "Excuse me, sir, do you have fifty cents?" Their names were Keffer (8) and Hugh (10). "I do have fifty cents and I'm willing to help you get your French fries, but I'd like you to help me with something too," I said to them. I then spoke to them about the gospel and the boys listened intently. It's important to remember that even though Belize (or any other country) proclaims to be a Christian country, I do not believe it is wise to assume that everyone is already saved.

After talking with them and hearing their testimony I was convinced that Keffer and Hugh understood the gospel and were genuine Christians. I then told them that if they agreed to give out ten gospel packets, then I would give them the fifty cents they needed. I felt that the boys would appreciate the money more if they had to earn it. They agreed and took ten gospel packets each. I then gave Kayla the fifty cents in order for them to get their French fries. Upon receiving the fries, I watched Keffer and Hugh proceeded down the street giving gospel packets away with one hand and munching on their fries with the other hand, and all three of us were rejoicing as they went their way. **PTL!**

> *"Tell of Jesus your Saviour! If His mercies you know,*
> *Show the light of His favor – Let the joy overflow."[21]*
>
> E.E. Hewitt & S.B. Jackson

It was after 4 pm and I was ready to head back to the pastor's home I was staying at in Belize after having an exciting day of soul winning. The pastor's wife was in the States visiting family and he was out doing errands, although we stayed in touch via cell phone. Earlier in the morning, he dropped me off in downtown Belize

City, and he told me how to get back to the house and so forth. In Belize City, much like many other nations, there is taxi service available. So I thanked Kayla and her staff for their hospitality and I walked a few blocks to where a taxi stand was. When I got there, it was not what I expected. These taxi drivers in Belize wore plain clothes and their cabs were not visibly identifiable from what I could see, so these cars didn't look like the cabs in New York or Boston that I'm used to. There were about four or five men standing in this little taxi stand corner which looked like a small parking lot. Nowhere did I see a "taxi stand" sign posted or anything like that, so thinking I was in the wrong place I turned to leave. "You need a taxi?" said a tall Jamaican man who had just come from around the corner. I told him I did and then I gave him the address I was staying at. To ride a taxi in America, you normally get in the back seat, and since that's what I'm accustomed to, I reached for the back door and just before I opened it, the man opened the front door and motioned me to sit up front. I was already nervous as I was in an unfamiliar area, I was alone, and I didn't know if I was really getting into a taxi cab, or if I was getting into a car of a tall mean-looking man, you wouldn't want to run into in an alley, whether day or night, if you know what I mean.

I thought he might drive me to a back alley or something and pull out a weapon and try to rob me. So I opened the front passenger door, got in and immediately I told him I was a preacher visiting from Boston as if to say, "Hey pal, I'm a servant of the Lord and if you harm me, you'll have to contend with Almighty God, and I wouldn't want to be you on that day!" After telling him I was a preacher, I gave him the address to the pastor's house, and then I did what I normally do when I'm a little nervous and want to break the ice with someone, I talked about the Lord! After talking for a minute, the driver told me his name was Alan, and he looked Jamaican because, in fact, as he told me, he moved from Jamaica to Belize City. Once we got on the main road and the area looked familiar again, my unwarranted fears disappeared as I realized that Alan was taking me in the right direction. Since I now knew where I was, I wouldn't have much time before we arrived at my destination, so I cut right to the chase and gave Alan the gospel. As I was explaining the good news to him, he told me to open his glove compartment, and when I did I found a Bible in there. "I read it in between jobs," he said. Although he had a Bible, he wasn't saved because he thought good works would get him to heaven. Alan also told me he was living with his girlfriend and they were not married. Now the temptation for me was to get off track into this side issue of him being an unmarried man living with his girlfriend. But I resisted that temptation because although that is sinful in God's eyes, it's more important to discuss salvation which is a person's greatest need.

BELIZE!

The pastor's house was further up on the main road we were on, and as it came into view, I did my best to make it clear to Alan that biblical salvation was not by works, but solely by faith in Christ and His finished work on the cross. As we pulled up to the pastor's home, I said a quick prayer for Alan. Then I paid Alan for the ride and handed him one of the few gospel packets I had left which included the church's contact information. He was in a hurry to get back to the taxi stand and get another customer, but before he drove off, he looked at me and said, "Thanks man, you gave me something to think about." God gave Alan something important to think about that day, but looking back at this incident that initially was nerve-racking for me I also had something to think about. In Mark 5:36 Jesus said, *"Be not afraid, only believe."* I realized that when you're in the will of God and you're doing a job for Him, you are invincible until you finish it and He's ready for you to come home to heaven. With that perspective, I can say as David said in Psalm 56:4 *"In God I will praise his word, in God I have put my trust; I will not fear what flesh can do unto me."* **PTL!**

> ***"The greatest privilege of earthly life is to give some fellow creature the blessed word of God"*[22]**
>
> J. A. Broadus

One morning the pastor I was staying with received a call from a lady who had just recently gotten saved at his church. She was requesting the pastor go visit her boyfriend named Doug in the hospital, so we headed there. The pastor had never met Doug before, so we didn't know what the man looked like or what to expect. When we got to the hospital, we got the room number from the front desk, but when we went to the room, we found out that Doug wasn't there. There had been a mix-up, and we had gotten the wrong information, as Doug was in actually in another room. Instead of finding Doug there in the first room we went to, we met a guy named Jude. The pastor left me with Jude and went to find in what room Doug was really staying. After some small talk and giving Jude my testimony, I asked: "Jude if you died tonight, do you know for sure you would go to heaven?" To this Jude replied, "I don't." It's clear from his answer that although Jude said had attended a church, he was not a Christian. So after giving the gospel, Jude allowed me, a visitor from the States the privilege of leading him to Christ. When I first came into Jude's room, he had a sad and gloomy countenance, but after he accepted Jesus as his Saviour his face just seemed to brighten up. A few minutes later the pastor came in and said he had found Doug, and Doug also came to trust Christ as his Saviour. It was exciting to think according to *our* plan I would not have met Jude that day, but in God's plan, I met him and with the Lord, there are no coincidences. That day was amazing, and it was just another

BELIZE!

reminder, we as Christians *get to* serve an amazing God. **PTL!**

> *"There is no joy in the world like the joy of bringing one soul to Christ."*[23]
>
> William Barclay

I made my way to my seat on my second of two consecutive flights, this one from Miami back to Boston. After my trip to Israel some time ago, Belize was an outstanding experience. I had stayed there for nearly two weeks and it felt like a day because the time went so fast. This flight wasn't that full. The rows in front and behind me were empty, and I thought my desire to have a passenger seated next to me wouldn't be fulfilled. After having nobody sitting near me on the previous return flight from Belize to Miami, I took a nap and enjoyed some much-needed sleep. But now I was energized and praying under my breath that there would be someone to have a redemptive conversation with. Much to my surprise, just when it seemed like nobody would come to sit near me, a woman came up the aisle, stored her luggage and sat in the seat next to me.

Other than a mere "hello," this woman had her headphones on and her face in some magazine and the thought of having a gospel-centered conversation was quickly fading away. Surely when the plane landed, I could give her a tract for the road, and although I believe tracts are effective, I also enjoy talking to people about the most important Person in my life, the Lord Jesus Christ. After the captain informed us that the plane reached an altitude of about 25,000 feet, the seat belt signs went off and the woman next to me took her earphones off and got up to go the direction of the restroom. Upon her return and seeing an open door, I said hello and talked to her about general things, trying to be folksy and break the ice. She told me her name was Debbie, and she was from Florida heading to Boston to visit her sister. I began the conversation and spoke of natural, earthly things and as the Holy Spirit led, I transitioned into spiritual things. I did this by pulling out one of the three remaining gospel tracts I had left for the trip. "Debbie, I only have a few of these left, and I'd like you to have one," I said. Then I gave my brief testimony and my reason for visiting Belize. I then went right into a gospel conversation with her. During our interaction, Debbie told me she already accepted Christ as her Saviour several years earlier. "That's awesome," I told her and then I shared with her the joy I receive when I get into redemptive conversations with people and take them through the gospel. There is no greater joy than to talk to someone about the person you are in a love relationship with! During our talk, I realized Debbie didn't have much experience verbally explaining the gospel to people, so I challenged her to start somewhere by taking a tract from me and use it to explain the gospel to someone the Lord brings to her. She agreed to take me up on my

BELIZE!

challenge and was very thankful that I took the time to gently *provoke* her to seek a higher level of joy and adventure in her walk with the Lord Jesus.

Our plane landed safely at Logan airport in Boston. I was back in the States after being away on a mission trip in Belize, but I had two more gospel tracts in my pocket I wanted to give out. Just as soon as I realized I was two tracts away from meeting my goal, God provided the two individuals to give them to. As I was walking up the aisle to exit the plane, I saw a stewardess at the door bidding people farewell, and then I saw a man dressed like he could be the pilot or co-pilot coming out of the cockpit area. As they greeted me and wished me farewell, I reached into my pocket, took out the two remaining tracts and said "Thanks for the smooth flight" and then handing them the tracts I said, "This is about another flight, the flight to heaven and I hope you'll be on that one." In response the stewardess said, "Amen, thank you so much" and the captain said, "Hey this is cool, thanks." As I waved them farewell I was thinking "Two more seeds planted!" Wherever and to whoever the Holy Spirit leads you to plant gospel seeds, just remember this. Your mission may not seem appealing to you initially, but when you go in faith, you'll be a co-laborer with your Heavenly Father and He'll always make it an adventure. **PTL!**

Conclusion

I wrote this book to help more of God's people to see the Great Commission as a fun adventure for the enjoying instead of just a duty to dread. My prayer is that God would give you eyes to see every day as a new possibility that will arouse in you a sense of wonder at every new face and every new situation God brings across your path. I challenge you, dear reader, to respond to God's invitation to seize the opportunities in front of you. As a child of the King, don't rob Him or yourself by living for less. Your opportunities are *many* and they are *now*! I hope my personal soul winning stories stirred you up to go dig up spiritual diamonds buried in the sands of lost souls out there. Now go trek the evangelism trail God has for you today for *His* glory and *your* blessing. On the next page, to equip you for your journey, I've compiled a list of helpful action steps I trust will be helpful.

Action Steps

I.   Realize that the mission field is *people*, not geography, and it begins outside your front door (not in a foreign country). *Prior* to going out to the field, get yourself familiar with the biblical evangelism strategy and Bible verses you plan on using to explain God's plan of salvation to the lost (for example Mark 1:15; John 1:12, 3:16; James 2:10; Heb 10:12; Rom 3:10, 6:23; 1st John 5:12-13; or Eph 2:8-9 etc.). *Remember* to use God's Law (the Commandments) to bring the knowledge of sin to their conscience (Rom 7:7, 13) so it can then work as a schoolmaster to help them see their need for Christ (Gal 3:24). **People must realize their lost condition before salvation will make sense to them!

II.   Equip yourself to sow the gospel seed to anyone; anywhere by having (in your bag, car, pockets, vehicle etc.), CDs, videos, booklets and/or plenty of tracts, preferably those people will most likely want to read (i.e. tracts from *EvanTell*, *Tract Planet* and other colorful, professionally designed ones). It's also important to have religion-specific tracts. **Also, where it's possible and appropriate, be ready to get the prospect's contact info and make sure any materials you give away have the contact info on it (yours or your church) for future follow up.

III.   If possible, find a soul winning partner for encouragement and accountability (i.e., Jesus sent out

His disciples by twos to set the Scriptural example - Luke10:1). But even if you can't and you're going solo, be sure to go filled with the Holy Spirit.

IV.   Realize that you save no one, you only plant or water the seed. God is the Saviour and the one who gives the increase (1st Cor 3:6-7). Soul fishing is *your* job, soul saving is *His* job. Keeping this perspective will help you avoid discouragement if faced with a poor response.

V.   Pray for and rely on God's power (Luke 24:49; Acts 1:8) and His leading as for *where* and to *whom* you should witness just like Philip did (Acts 8:26-29). Ask the Lord for divine appointments and then be sensitive to them. Also ask Him to help you genuinely love people without conditions, regardless of their response to the gospel. People are souls to be won to Christ, not trophies to be collected and put on a shelf.

VI.   Ask the Lord to give you and your church new and *creative* ways to evangelize (such as some mentioned in this book).

VII.   Though we aren't *of* the world, we're still *in* the world, so like Paul, let's seek to become all things to all men to win as many as possible (1st Cor 9:19-22). This doesn't mean we change the message (the gospel) but as Paul did, we must contextualize (adapt our approach to delivering the message) based on where and who our audience is. It's wise to notice how the JWs and

ACTION STEPS

Mormons dress when they're out there trying to get converts. What these cults wear helps the public spot them coming from a mile away and it makes it easier for people to avoid or ignore them. Except for their false doctrine, we can learn from the mistakes of their approach and be wise as serpents and harmless as doves (Matt 10:16). Is it wise to wear the same clothing while fishing, which they would require you to wear in a court of law? Try not to be out of touch or out of date with how you dress and speak or you'll cease to be relatable to those you need to reach. How we approach people should be less about copying 18th century Victorian Era *formalism* and more about modern-day *realism*. Jesus related to the everyday *common folk* (Mark 12:37). Let's do likewise.

VIII. Though we have a message to deliver and we don't want to get sidetracked onto other topics, let's remember that soul winning is really more of a *conversation* than a one-sided *presentation*. Jesus had a genuine *conversation* with the Samaritan woman (John 4). He should be our example.

IX. Check out these helpful website resources that have blessed me as they showcase more examples of how God is working in and through those who step out in faith to be His witnesses:

- Mark Cahill Ministries newsletter at www.markcahill.org

- Chick Publications *Battle Cry* newsletter at www.Chick.com/bc

- Baptist International Missions Inc., *World Magazine* at www.Bimi.org/worldmag

- http://www.evantell.org/stories

And now...

X. **Go out there, *expecting* to be amazed!**

Endnotes

Chapter 1

1. Charles H. Spurgeon, *Spurgeon's Maxims for Living*, www.spurgeon.us/mind_and_heart/quotes/s4.htm

2. R.A. Torrey, http://thegatheringplacehome.myfastforum.org/archive/quotes-by-famous-preachers__o_t__t_3107.html

Chapter 2

3. Billy Sunday, *Famous Preacher Quotes*, www.forgottenword.org/quotes.html

Chapter 3

4. Ron Luce, http://harvestministry.org/100-mission-mottos

5. Lester Roloff, *Words Fitly Spoken* p. 34

6. C.L. Cagan, www.rlhymersjr.com/online_sermons/2011/0123am_blessingsofsoulwinner.html

7. Francis Dixon, www.wordsoflife.co.uk/bible-studies/study-9-the-soul-winner%C2%92s-reward/

8. C.T. Studd, www.proverbs2525.org/collections/quotes_missions.php

9. D. L. Moody, www.soulwinning.info/gs/quotes.htm

10. C.T. Studd, www.wholesomewords.org/missions/msquotes.html

11. Charles H. Spurgeon, *Serving the Lord With Gladness #769*, www.spurgeongems.org/vols13-15/vols13-15.htm

EVANGELISM'S FLIPSIDE

12. J. Campbell White, *The Laymen's Missionary Movement*, 1909, http://gracetabernacle.org/gracelife/quotes/service-encouragement.htm

Chapter 4

13. Alexander Maclaren, http://christianquotes.org/tag/cat/125

Chapter 5

14. William Carey, *The Missionary Herald*, The Baptist Magazine 1843; Vol. 35, p.41

15. Charles H. Spurgeon, *Serving the Lord with Gladness #769*, www.spurgeongems.org/vols13-15/vols13-15.htm

16. J. Campbell White, *The Laymen's Missionary Movement*, 1909, http://gracetabernacle.org/gracelife/quotes/service-

Chapter 6

17. Charles H. Spurgeon, *Serving the Lord with Gladness #769*, www.spurgeongems.org/vols13-15/vols13-15.htm

Chapter 7

18. Karen Watson, www.finestquotes.com/select_quote-category-Missionaries-page-0.htm

Chapter 8

19. Adoniram Judson, http://christian-quotes.ochristian.com/The-Future-Quotes/page-5.shtml

20. Frank C. Huston, *It Pays to Serve Jesus,* Soul Stirring Songs & Hymns, Sword of the Lord Publishers; 1972; p.386

21. E.E. Hewitt & S.B. Jackson, *Let the Joy Overflow*, Soul Stirring Songs & Hymns, Sword of the Lord Publishers; 1972, p.199

22. J.A. Broadus, *Famous Preacher Quotes*, www.forgottenword.org/quotes.html

ENDNOTES

23. William Barclay, http://gracetabernacle.org/gracelife/quotes/evangelism-joy.htm

About the Author

John "Jay" Ricci has earned an undergraduate degree from a public university as well as a theological degree from a Bible college. Since the Lord clearly called him into evangelism over fifteen years ago, Jay has been preaching and teaching using a variety of creative and engaging methods in churches, parks, public events, jails, nursing homes, airports, subways, college campuses and everywhere else in the US and in other countries as the Lord leads. Jay also has experience leading an addictions recovery ministry as well as teaching youth and adult Sunday school classes. He currently lives and ministers in the Boston, MA area.

If the author can be of further service you may contact him through his blog:

jjrbiblepreachingandteaching.wordpress.com

www.ingramcontent.com/pod-product-compliance
Lightning Source LLC
Chambersburg PA
CBHW071731040426
42446CB00011B/2316